Table of Contents

	Page
DISCLAIMER	i
EXECUTIVE SUMMARY	ii
PREFACE	iv
INTRODUCTION	1
THE IMPACT OF THE PAST AND PRESENT: WHY DOJ AND DHS	1
DOJ	3
ATF	4
DEA	5
FBI	6
DHS	7
ICE	8
LESSONS ON UNIFICATION	9
National Security Act of 1947	10
Goldwater Nichols DOD Reorganization Act of 1987	10
THE INTERAGENCY CROSSROADS	12
Gangs	12
Transnational Crime	14
Explosives Investigations	15
Arson	16
Terrorism Prevention	16
RECOMMENDATIONS	17
Organizational Capital	18
Human Capital	19
Resource Capital	20
CONCLUSIONS	21
BIBLIOGRAPHY	23
ENDNOTES	28

Preface

It was my intent in this work to submit ideas for further consideration on the dynamic subject of national security and the harmonized role of federal law enforcement agencies. The motive for me in this endeavor lay in a desire to add objectively to the field of academic study on this subject. In preparation for the work that led to this narrative I received valuable assistance from a number of dedicated people. My search for source material at the incipient stages of this study was enhanced greatly by the skilled research staff of the United States Marine Corps, Gray Research Center, whom I must first acknowledge. The Marine Corps University, Command and Staff College (CSC), including its knowledgeable professors and dynamic curriculum were equally enriching. I am also grateful to the students from Conference Group Six, all of whom provided valuable perspectives through many seminar discussions. Especially, I thank Dr. Francis H. Marlo, my academic mentor, whose skillful guidance is greatly appreciated. Finally, to my wife and family who supported me throughout these academic pursuits, I am wholeheartedly thankful.

Introduction Section

"We the People of the United States, in Order to form a more perfect Union, establish Justice, insure domestic Tranquility, provide for the common defense, promote the general Welfare, and secure the Blessing of Liberty to ourselves and our Posterity...."[1]

—The Preamble to the Constitution of the United State

In response to the terrorist strikes of September 11, 2001, (9-11) Congress created the Department of Homeland Security (DHS) to have, as stated by President George W. Bush, "the agencies accountable for protecting the country under one roof."[2] More than 10 years later key security functions are still controlled by separate agencies under disparate department "roofs," even as threats associated with domestic and international crime and terrorism have increased. Additionally, today's economic climate requires greater interagency efficiency because of more limited U.S. government budgets. At the forefront of the nation's security are the United States (U.S.) federal law enforcement agencies from the Departments of Justice (DOJ) and Homeland Security (DHS). A 2011 Government Accountability Office (GAO) study recommended more effective collaboration between DOJ and DHS "to combat terrorism and fight existing and emerging criminal threats."[3] To meet the needs posed by today's national security environment and constrained economy, America's federal law enforcement sector must undergo legislative changes to coordinate investigations more effectively, foster a collaborative culture, and promote cost-effective practices.

The Impact of the Past and Present: Why DOJ and DHS?

In the history of the U.S., the federal law enforcement (FLE) sector has undergone a great number of institutional changes to meet the nation's needs. Guiding these changes has been and is the most basic purpose of government: to provide for the security of its citizens. In *Federalist No. 3*, John Jay states that concept as follows:

> "Among the many objects to which a wise and free people find it necessary to direct their attention, that of providing for their safety seems to be the first....I mean only to consider it as it respects the security for the preservation of peace and tranquillity, as well as against dangers from foreign arms and influences, as from dangers of the like kind arising from domestic causes."[4]

The U.S. today faces complex and long-term security needs and a challenging fiscal outlook. Additionally, one important concept has influenced the nature of that sector and underscored the importance of interagency effectiveness and unity of effort. That concept–national security–provides a base of influence relevant today and is derived from the National Security Act of 1947. National security was introduced into the American lexicon as a result of that Act, in part because it created the National Security Council.

The National Security Strategy describes national security today in terms of providing for the safety of America from foreign threats.[5] As stated by President Barack Obama:

> "Our Armed Forces will always be a cornerstone of our security, but they must be complemented. Our security also depends upon diplomats who can act in every corner of the world, from grand capitals to dangerous outposts; development experts who can strengthen governance and support human dignity; and intelligence and law enforcement that can unravel plots, strengthen justice systems, and work seamlessly with other countries."[6]

Accordingly, FLE agencies play an important role relating to the security of the nation. This national security role is particularly critical with those agencies whose missions entail combating violent crime linked to transnational criminal organizations (TCOs) and terrorism. That importance is emphasized by a 2003 Library of Congress analytical report that identified concerns about arms smuggling, drug cartels, and known terrorist groups in Mexico.[7] Combating these concerns also require adequate fiscal resources at a time when pressure is on Congress to reduce spending and address the looming U.S. national debt.

All federal government agencies face constrained budgets for years to come due to long-term budgetary shortfalls, and therefore must operate with greater efficiency. In 2007 Congressional testimony, Comptroller General for the U.S. David M. Walker stated that America's "…current fiscal path would gradually erode, if not suddenly damage, our economy, our standard of living, and ultimately our domestic tranquility and national security."[8] While this report is over five years old, current austerity measures are expected for years to come. In August 2011, Congress passed the Budget Control Act of 2011, which requires significant reductions of government spending through 2021.[9]

Four DOJ and DHS law enforcement agencies serve key and interrelated roles associated with America's security. The strategic importance of these agencies has evolved as a result of landmark legislation over two centuries. Each agency's current areas of jurisdictional responsibility is rooted in these legislative origins and today they operate in a common law enforcement "jurisdictional-crossroads," due to similarities in their enforcement programs in connection with transnational crime, violent crime within the nation, and terrorism. Those agencies are the Bureau of Alcohol, Tobacco, Firearms and Explosives (ATF); the Drug Enforcement Administration (DEA); and the Federal Bureau of Investigation (FBI), all from DOJ; and Immigration and Customs Enforcement (ICE) from DHS.

DOJ: An executive department of the U.S. government, DOJ serves to enforce the federal laws and ensure the administration of justice and public safety. Today DOJ comprises forty-two sections including the following major components:

> "These include the United States Attorneys, who prosecute offenders and represent the United States Government in court; the National Security Division, which coordinates the Department's highest priority of combating terrorism and protecting national security; [and] the major investigative agencies – the Federal Bureau of Investigations; the Drug Enforcement Administrations; and the Bureau of Alcohol, Tobacco, Firearms and Explosives – which prevent and deter crime and arrest criminal suspects…"[10]

DOJ's beginnings are traced to 1789 when the U.S. Judiciary Act established the first Attorney General (AG). However the Act limited the capabilities of that position. In 1870, the Act to Establish the Department of Justice created DOJ as an Executive Department headed by the AG. With the 1870 Act, DOJ was charged with the principal responsibilities of prosecuting the U.S. laws and providing control over the country's federal law enforcement agencies.

ATF: In 2003, when it was renamed the Bureau of Alcohol, Tobacco, Firearms and Explosives, ATF was transferred from the Department of Treasury to the Department of Justice as a result of the Homeland Security Act (HSA). ATF today combats violent crime and criminal organizations by enforcing the federal laws relating to "…the illegal use and trafficking of firearms, the illegal use and storage of explosives, acts of arson and bombings, acts of terrorism, and the illegal diversion of alcohol and tobacco products."[11] ATF operates offices throughout the U.S. as well as in Mexico, El Salvador, Colombia, Canada, and Iraq, and it has a representative at Interpol Headquarters, Lyon, France. ATF is also involved in efforts to combat TCOs in Mexico and Latin America; the illicit use of firearms by narcotics traffickers, violent criminals and illicit gangs; the investigation of bombings and the criminal use of fires; and other similar crimes. The work force of ATF totals more than 5,000 personnel.

ATF considers its origins to date back to the first U.S. Congress, which imposed taxes on spirits to pay debts associated with the Revolutionary War. The Act's administration fell to the Department of the Treasury (Treasury). From 1863 to the era of Prohibition, ATF's responsibilities related to organized crime and tax evasion through its predecessor in Treasury's Internal Revenue Service (IRS).[12] The IRS' Prohibition Unit, a predecessor of ATF, was formed as a result of the Volstead Act to combat violent criminal organizations during Prohibition, and from that time onward ATF's primary responsibilities included combating violent criminal acts.

From the 1930s through the present, ATF has investigated criminal acts carried out with firearms and explosives, especially when linked to violent crime. This mission included enforcing the National Firearms Act of 1934, which targeted the illegal use of certain firearms by regulating machine guns, shotguns and rifles with short barrels, silencers and certain other weapons, through the imposition of a Treasury tax and registration requirement.[13] ATF was later charged with broader firearms jurisdiction as a result of the Federal Firearms Act of 1938. The 1938 Act, later amended by the Gun Control Act of 1968, also made it a federal crime to sell or possess a firearm by a prohibited person, regulated all U.S. gun dealers, and added to ATF's jurisdiction the enforcement of laws relating to explosives devices. Title XI of the Organized Crime Control Act in 1970 and the Safe Explosives Act in 2002 directed ATF to enforce additional laws associated with explosives and to regulate the explosives industry.[14]

DEA: The current mission of DEA entails the investigation and prosecution of large-scale drug traffickers of interest to the U.S. This enforcement mission primarily involves illicit interstate and international narcotics operations. DEA plays a prominent role in America's national security scheme through its counterdrug strategies. These law enforcement strategies are applied internationally, particularly in Central America, South America, and Mexico. For example, as announced by U.S. Attorney Laura Duffy, Southern District of California, DEA played a lead investigative role resulting in the January 4, 2012, guilty plea of Benjamin Arellano-Felix, the leader of the Tijuana Cartel/Arellano Felix Organization, in U.S. Federal District Court.[15] DEA has nearly 10,000 employees and staff's offices domestically and in 65 countries.[16]

DEA links its roots to the Department of Treasury, Bureau of Internal Revenue, which inaugurated the U.S. federal drug law enforcement era in 1915. However, DEA's most direct heritage began many years later.[17] In the early nineteen-seventies, the U.S. administration recognized that federal drug enforcement efforts had become a problem due to nearly 60 years of fragmented policies. As a result, in 1973, an Executive Order (EO) of President Nixon unified five agencies into the newly created DEA. That EO merged DEA's predecessor, Bureau of Narcotics and Dangerous Drugs (BNDD), which had become "the primary drug law enforcement agency," with four additional agencies into DEA.[18]

FBI: The FBI's responsibilities consist of law enforcement and intelligence community functions to protect the U.S. As shaped by the events of 9-11, FBI's top three priorities became the protection of the U.S. from terrorist attack, foreign intelligence operations and espionage, and cyber-based attacks and high technology crimes.[19] Other priorities include fighting public corruption; protecting civil rights; and combating transnational/national criminal organizations and enterprises, white-collar crime, and significant violent crime.[20] As of November 2011, FBI maintains a workforce of over 35,000 and has offices domestically and in 60 international locations.[21]

The historical roots of the FBI span a century in which its prominence in America's federal law enforcement and intelligence schemes grew due to an expansion of its responsibilities in fighting crime. Formed in 1908, FBI's forerunner, Bureau of Investigations (BOI) was conceived as a dedicated component of DOJ to combat interstate crimes.[22] BOI started with just 10 prior employees of Treasury's Secret Service and a few more from the DOJ.[23] The nineteen-thirties played a defining role, for Congress passed a federal kidnapping law in response to the highly publicized kidnapping of Charles Lindbergh's baby and assigned its enforcement to the FBI.

During World War II (WWII), the FBI uncovered spy rings pursuant to newly assigned authorities from President Roosevelt relating to "[s]ubversion, sabotage, and espionage..."[24] The enforcement of several new federal statutes were assigned to FBI in the 1960s to combat civil rights violations, racketeering, and gambling.[25] Congress additionally passed the Racketeer Influenced and Corrupt Organization (RICO) Statute of 1970. A section of this law then provided federal agents, including those from FBI, means to pursue enterprises involved in illicit acts such as arson, robbery, extortion, murder, and narcotics trafficking. The FBI shifted its priorities in the 1980s, first to combat a sharp rise in drug trafficking in the America, then in concert with an expansion of its "...jurisdiction to cover terrorist acts against U.S. citizens outside the U.S. boundaries."[26] By the 1990s a confluence of events—the end of the Cold War and a significant rise in U.S. crime and violence—prompted FBI to reallocate substantial resources, including special agents, by shifting priorities from foreign counterintelligence to the enforcement of violent crime.[27] Finally, as stated above, the FBI shifted its priorities anew to eight primary areas, following the 9-11 terrorist strikes in the U.S. homeland.[28]

DHS: The Homeland Security Act of 2002 (HSA 2002) represented an expansive endeavor that created DHS, due to security needs resulting from the 9-11 terrorist attacks in America. HSA 2002 reforms were expansive because of the scope of mandated changes; it established DHS as a cabinet level component that unified 22 former separate agencies under its command.[29] For President Bush, HSA 2002 and the creation of DHS were reminiscent of the National Security Act of 1947, another large-scale government reformation at the Cold War's beginning.[30] The overarching objective of DHS today "...is to ensure a homeland that is safe, secure and resilient against terrorism...."[31] Core mission functions support this objective. DHS defines these functions as follows: "1. Preventing terrorism and enhancing security; 2. [s]ecuring and managing our borders; 3. [e]nforcing and administering our immigration laws; 4. [s]afeguarding and securing cyberspace; [and] 5. [e]nsuring resilience to disasters...."[32] The large number of diverse agencies within DHS has resulted in organizational challenges. A CATO Institute report in 2011 found that, "DHS has too many subdivisions in too many disparate fields to operate effectively..." and also cited past Congressional concerns recorded during hearings leading up to the passing of HSA 2002.[33]

ICE: ICE serves as a unique component of DHS, because it serves as the principal law enforcement branch of that department. As stated by ICE, its primary mission "...is to promote homeland security and public safety through criminal and civil enforcement of federal laws governing border control, customs, trade, and immigration."[34] This mission spans two principal directorates: Homeland Security Investigations (HSI) and Enforcement and Removal Operations (ERO). Combined, these components comprise more than 20,000 personnel, making ICE the "...second largest investigative agency in the federal government."[35]

ICE (HSI) employs enforcement resources and strategies that are similar to aspects of many of the enforcement resources and initiatives of ATF, DEA, and FBI. These include investigations associated with narcotics and firearms trafficking across U.S. borders, transnational criminal organizations, cybercrime, gang activity in the U.S., and counterterrorism efforts.[36] In particular, U.S. counter drug strategies and transnational crime have made all four agencies prominent in law enforcement efforts against the Mexican cartels. HSI organizational resources include an intelligence branch and an international affairs office with special agents assigned to over 47 countries.[37]

The history of ICE dates back to the founding of the U.S. and has evolved since that time according to the nations needs. The Fifth Act of Congress, in 1789, first established a federal agency to collect taxes on imported goods, that agency soon became the U.S. Customs Service (USCS), the predecessor of ICE.[38] Through the eighteen-fifties, the USCS was involved primarily with regulating the taxation of imports.[39] Through the end of the nineteenth-century, USCS also filled growing regulatory needs associated with immigration. In the twentieth-century, interdiction programs relating especially to drugs, money laundering, child pornography, and illicit exportations (including firearms) took on more emphasis.

As can be seen above, the FLE sector has experienced over two centuries of change in order to address America's criminal enforcement needs and address threats to its security. Legislation accounted for many of these changes and as a result defined the responsibilities of newly created departments and agencies. The changes brought on by FLE's heritage have, today, formed a "crossroads of responsibilities" because four key agencies share similar jurisdictional responsibilities in support of the nations security. These agencies, ATF, DEA, FBI, and ICE (HSI), all serve key roles in keeping America safe from transnational crime, violent crime inside the country, and the prevention of terrorism.

Lessons on Unification

Establishing an effective level of interagency coordination between the U.S. military services required many decades of legislative change spanning from the World War II (WWII) era to the Goldwater-Nichols Department of Defense (DOD) Reorganization Act of 1986 (GNA). An intense need for collaboration between the U.S. military services during WWII and unified counsel to the President led to the creation of the Joint Chiefs of Staff (JCS). In 1942, President Roosevelt employed the JCS as an informal body represented by both services. The JCS proved ineffective in unifying the services, such as with America's war in the Pacific or institutionalizing joint practices, because Roosevelt "...never issued an order describing their roles or powers."[40] The disparate interests of the service chiefs hindered ultimately a central and strategic course of action. Army General George C. Marshal and JCS member "…believed that unity of command in the various theaters of war needed to extend to Washington as well—in the form of a single chief of staff who could resolve disputes among the military and assign clear priorities for plans and budgets."[41] At the end of WWII, the need for change among the military services was heightened due to America's enhanced and global security role, its possession of atomic bombs and the need for post-WWII stability in Europe.

National Security Act (NSA) of 1947: The NSA of 1947 and its subsequent amendments were touted as important changes to unify the U.S. military, but they were ill fated. On July 25, 1947, President Harry S. Truman, signed the Act into law. In his memoirs he described the conditions that prompted the change:

> "It had been evident to me, from the record of the Pearl Harbor hearings, that the tragedy was as much the result of the inadequate military system which provided for no unified command, either in the field or in Washington, as it was the personal failure of Army or Navy commanders."[42]

Truman considered the 1947 Act a great accomplishment; however it "…was not as strong as the original proposal sent to Congress, since it included concessions on both sides for the sake of bringing together the Army and Navy."[43] Changes to the 1947 Act in 1949, 1953, and 1958, aimed to raise the services' unified capabilities by strengthening the authorities of the Secretary of Defense and changing the JCS structure. Unfortunately effective collaboration was never achieved. A government study in the late 1970s reported on the command structure of the military and found that the JCS had "a limited role in defense policy,…and that it needs a major overhaul," a powerful indictment presented to President Jimmy Carter.[44]

Goldwater-Nichols Department of Defense Reorganization Act of 1986 (GNA): The GNA succeeded in reforming DOD because it designed an organization that synchronized the efforts of the different services. Congress recognized that national defense plans did not represent the harmonized ground, maritime, and air strategies of the Army, Navy and Air Force respectively; because those strategies resulted in ineffective prioritization and the allocation of resources.[45] Capping these reasons for change, the Congress and the American public witnessed several U.S. military operational failures in the nineteen-seventies and eighties, including the Vietnam War, the 1980 failed attempt to rescue 52 hostages in Iran, and aspects of the invasion of Grenada. An established defense analyst summarizes the reasons for these setbacks by stating as follows: "These failures had a number of common denominators—poor military advice to political leaders, lack of unity of command, and inability to operate jointly."[46]

The GNA of 1986 improved inter-service and DOD unity, because it mandated strategic, operational, and administrative reforms. The reforms initiated by Congress were guided by broad intents found in the 1986 Act, including the following:

(1) "to reorganize the Department of Defense and strengthen civilian authority in the Department;
(2) to improve the military advice provided to the president, the National Security Council, and the Secretary of Defense;
(3) to place clear responsibility on the commanders of the unified and specified combatant commands for the accomplishment of missions assigned to those commands;
(4) to ensure that the authority of the commanders of the unified and specified combatant commands is fully commensurate with the responsibility of those commanders for the accomplishment of missions assigned to their commands;
(5) to increase attention to the formulation of strategy and to contingency planning;
(6) to provide for more efficient use of defense resources;
(7) to improve joint officer management policies; and
(8) otherwise to enhance the effectiveness of military operations and improve the management and administration of the Department of Defense."[47]

Most studies today reflect that the GNA was very effective. Lessons learned from failed operations prior to the GNA served as bases for inspiring joint planning doctrine, both on the strategic and operational level. General Norman Schwarzkopf, on the Gulf War said that,

"Goldwater-Nichols established very clear lines of command authority and responsibilities over subordinate commanders, and that meant a much more effective fighting force."[48]

The Interagency Crossroads Challenge

Current challenges facing the four DOJ and DHS agencies include overlapping areas of jurisdictional responsibilities, which have created competing interests and a need for more collaborative practices. These disparate interests have undermined unity of effort and increased operating costs. In each case of inefficient jurisdictional coordination, ambiguity related to the interagency roles and responsibilities is involved. In particular, improved collaboration is needed between ATF, DEA, FBI, and ICE-HSI in connection with the following enforcement categories: gangs, transnational crime, explosives, arson, and terrorism prevention.

Gangs:

Anti-gang initiatives between the DOJ and DHS agencies have resulted in disunity, because of a lack of one central federal law enforcement policy, complexity of a large number of disparate law enforcement anti-gang task forces, and lack of a central information sharing system. Effective enforcement associated with gangs is important because of the violence associated with these illicit groups in the U.S. The National Gang Intelligence Center assessed that in 2011 there were 1.4 million gang members in the U.S. (including the District of Colombia and Puerto Rico) in more than 33,000 gangs, and that these gangs accounted for 48% to 90% of the violent crime in most jurisdictions.[49] Gangs are found in all fifty U.S. states, and some are associated with Mexican TCOs as enforcers and drug smugglers across the U.S-Mexico border.[50]

In 2009, the GAO reviewed the anti-gang efforts between the DHS and DOJ agencies, and found that better coordination was needed between them due to disparate "...roles, responsibilities, and missions of headquarter-level gang coordination entities...."[51] The GAO studied and compared disparate task forces and supporting programs including: ATF's Violent Crime Impact Teams (VCIT); FBI's Violent Gang Safe Streets Task Force (SSTF); DEA's Metropolitan Enforcement Team (MET); and ICE's Operation Community Shield Program. The study found that the agencies needed to "enhance their collaboration in combating gangs [relating especially to] differentiation of roles and responsibilities ..." and that by strengthening their efforts it would "...reduce gaps, or unnecessary overlaps."[52] The study also identified a need for greater inclusion of ICE during the formation of DOJ-based task forces in order to improve collaboration.[53]

In another study, uncoordinated anti-gang initiatives were identified between the DOJ and DHS interagency group. This study resulted in a May 2011 GAO report on interagency disagreements relating to crossover jurisdiction in the areas of "drugs, firearms, fugitives, gangs, arson, and explosives," where a surveyed FBI special agent stated that:

> "DEA, ATF, FBI, USMS [United States Marshalls Service] and Immigrations and Customs Enforcement...all work drug, gang, and firearms violations....[and] the roles are not clear, which has lead to duplication of efforts."[54]

The study was national in scope and involved completed surveys from 260 field-level agents originating from ATF, DEA, FBI, and USMS, and of those nearly 80% from members of the first three agencies.[55] More than 1/3 of the survey respondents stated that they experienced disagreements as a direct result of "unclear roles and responsibilities and a lack of information sharing related to their investigations as the cause."[56] When asked specifically about joint-agency drug and gang investigations, 30% and 42% of the respondents respectively, indicated a lack of clarity or only being partially clear relating to their roles and responsibilities.[57]

Another example entails efforts to combat multi-national gangs. Two particularly prominent gangs, MS-13 and M-18, are investigated by all four DOJ and DHS agencies;

however better coordination is needed between the agencies. ATF investigates violent acts associated with these gangs when a firearm or explosives is used, while DEA targets their narcotics trafficking aspects. The FBI approaches the effort broadly from an organized crime aspect, and ICE targets illicit activity associated with the border, including crimes by alien gang members. A Congressional Research Service study in 2010 emphasized the need for more enhanced information-sharing databases to support such investigations and identified the probable need for bilateral agreements with relevant countries in Latin America to combat these multi-national gangs.[58]

Transnational Crime:

Each of the DOJ and DHS agencies possess important investigative strengths that are made stronger when harmonized to combat TCOs based in Mexico. However, this synchronization is not consistent. TCOs in Mexico comprise large- and small- scale criminal organizations engaged in narcotics, cash, and human trafficking across the U.S. border. TCOs have emerged as significant criminal threats to both the U.S. and Mexico, causing record levels of violence, including murders, in Mexico. The negative influence of TCOs is also felt strongly at the national political level in Mexico. For example, in January 2012 the Washington Post reported that the impact of drug gangs in Mexico have risen to the point at which they have prompted concerns relating to their negative and corruptive influence on that country's Presidential election process in 2012.[59]

The four DOJ and DHS agencies combat illicit TCO activity according to respective mission-driven priorities, which result in disparate strategies that emphasize the need for close coordination to reach a more unified national objective. This more integrated approach, however, is not always achieved. For instance, ATF and ICE have worked to stem the flow of illegal weapons into Mexico, however the effectiveness of these efforts could be improved by more closely aligned strategies and sustained coordination. A July 2009 GAO study relating to coordinated ATF and ICE efforts to combat arms trafficking to Mexico illustrated that point as follows:

> "the agencies were not taking sufficient advantage of each other's expertise to more effectively carry out operations, such as ATF's expertise in firearms identification and [investigative techniques,]...and ICE's experience dealing with export violations and combating money laundering and alien smuggling...."[60]

Explosives Investigations:

The investigation of federal explosives and arson cases between ATF and FBI has resulted in conflicts due primarily to competing efforts to control those investigations. Both agencies have concurrent jurisdiction regarding these violations. The source of conflict is linked to the motive of the violation and how each agency approaches differently those cases. The FBI tends to approach these types of cases as probable terrorism, a characterization that reflects its number one priority, preventing terrorism; whereas ATF approaches these cases as a criminal act, which may have a link to terrorism. For example, conflict arose between the agencies in May 2007 during the investigation of a homemade bomb found at Liberty University in Virginia. The bomb had been found in a car the day prior to the funeral of Jerry Falwell, when after two days of witness interviews by ATF, "FBI tried to take over citing domestic terrorism."[61] The differences in this case were eventually worked out, but this clash prompted concerns, as reported in the Washington Post.[62]

In 2004 and 2008 DOJ tried, with some success, to clarify the roles of each agency, but some ambiguities still exist regarding agency roles.[63] A 2009 DOJ, Office of the Inspector General (OIG) report found that:

> "ATF believed it should have primacy because explosives enforcement...are inherent

functions of its central mission; FBI considered it to be the lead agency because it should determine whether an explosives incident has a nexus to terrorism making it a matter exclusively for the FBI to investigate….The FBI and ATF recognize that few explosives incidents are terrorism-related."[64]

Arson:

ATF and FBI responses to arson cases result in challenging scenarios, similar to those involving explosives investigations, when the incident's motive is not apparent. For instance shouting erupted between ATF and FBI at a 2004 fire scene of a subdivision in Charles County, Maryland, when eco-terrorism was alleged by the latter.[65] "Five men were ultimately convicted of setting the fires, and eco-terrorism was ruled out….[however not before issues had been aired publicly]….Arguments at similar fires flared more than a dozen times across the country in recent years," as reported in a Washington Post article.[66]

Terrorism Prevention:

There have been many successes in connection with preventing acts of terrorism in America over the past decade, however for the DOS and DHS agencies these effort must be sustained and wherever possible, enhanced through effective collaboration. The importance of counterterrorism efforts by the DOJ and DHS was underscored in a June 2011 report by the Heritage Foundation, "Since 9-11, at least 39 terror plots against the United States have been foiled," as well as at least seven additional plots in New York, Washington D.C., Los Angeles and Texas."[67] All four DOJ and DHS agencies span a broad area connected to counterterrorism and their federal law enforcement roles.

DOJ's primary objective is the prevention of terrorism. To that end, its law enforcement components, specifically FBI, DEA, and ATF, support that objective in concert with their respective missions. The FBI serves as the primary agency leading counterterrorism efforts and employs a multi-agency task force through its Joint Terrorism Task Force (JTTF) domestically to achieve that goal, while also maintaining a robust foreign presence. DEA and ATF also have foreign country presence and combat terrorism through counter narcotics strategies and by investigating violent crime and bombings in the U.S. Finally, DHS' mission, in which ICE-HSI plays a significant role, is primarily the prevention of terrorism in the homeland, especially acts linked to the U.S. borders.

The DOJ and DHS agencies face various challenges, including cultural factors, which have inhibited the best of collaborative efforts. FBI Director Robert Mueller, in a December 2011 Congressional oversight hearing, faced questions relating to FBI's inability to cooperate as well with DHS as a local police department and the role of management in improving cultural influences. He acknowledged that interagency collaboration has been a challenge for the FBI but emphasized that it has been elevated to one of their top priorities.[68] Another example of the continuing need for effective collaboration was illustrated in a 2007 GAO report as follows:

> "ATF was used only occasionally by the FBI as a counterterrorism resource prior to the 9-11 terrorist attacks despite its expertise….ATF's laboratories, investigators, and analysis were critical to the investigation of the February 1993 bombing of the World Trade Center and the April 1995 bombing of the Alfred P. Murrah Federal Building in Oklahoma City."[69]

Recommendations

Key federal law enforcement agencies today must adapt to perform in a highly synchronized enforcement environment to meet twenty-first century threats, which emanate from inside and outside U.S. borders. These agencies—including ATF, DEA, FBI, and ICE (HSI)—lead individually efforts to combat violent domestic crime and prevent terrorism. However, it will require legislative change by Congress to create an interagency environment that will harmonize the individual capabilities of the respective agencies and bring about a more powerful, cost-efficient, and collaborative capability. Prospective improvements among these agencies structures and administrations are not without precedence, for decades of DOD reforms have provided many valuable lessons for the law enforcement community to consider. Richard Chaney and Bill Taylor characterized these periods of transformation as follows:

> "Unity of command and effort has been a cardinal principle of successful military organizations throughout history. Coaxing that coordinated effort out of the separate armed services with different cultures and command structures always has been a challenge for U.S. [government and] military leaders"[70]

The following recommended reforms are designed to breakdown the complexities, which exists as barriers to more effective collaboration. These proposed changes intend to modernize the four DOJ and DHS agencies to meet the challenges of today, and include three areas for change: Organizational Capital, Human Capital, and Resource Capital.

Organizational Capital

The formation of a Joint Law Enforcement Team (JLET) will serve as the cornerstone of the proposed changes and will enable administrative oversight of investigative programs having joint interest between ATF, DEA, FBI, and ICE. The composition of the JLET specifies a chief who will alternate between DOJ and DHS, with the other agency holding the position of deputy chief. Both positions will be two-year assignments and be filled by deputy department level officials. The department providing the active chief position also will provide a small administrative staff. Additionally, the JLET will include one senior executive (SES-level) from each agency (ATF, DEA, FBI, and ICE) who will meet at least weekly to provide oversight of collaborative efforts among the four DOS and DHS agencies including major joint investigations. Additionally, the JLET will control special investigative funds issued to the individual agencies in concert with joint investigative efforts. The control of funds must be linked to U.S. national objectives, which are supported by the respective and coordinated enforcement programs of the DOJ and DHS agencies.

Finally, performance measures for each department and each agency must include, as an element of respective internal operational inspections, a way to rate the quality of unity of effort and collaboration among these agencies. A special review team comprising of representatives from DOJ and DHS Office of Inspector General should conduct the inspection jointly every three years. In order to assess accurately the level of interagency efficiency, program inspections need to perform comprehensive interviews of employees. These employees must fall within a varied rank structure including field agents, supervisors, and executive personnel, to allow for different perspectives relating to the study. For example, A GAO study conducted in 2011 found that:

> "DOJ components conduct inspections of offices every 3 to 6 years, which cover areas such as working relationships, operational programs, leadership, and management. However, officials from three of four component inspection divisions GAO interviewed said that they rely on interviews with senior management, such as the highest official in the field office, to gauge coordination and the working relationship among the DOJ law enforcement components, and do not solicit input from [lower-level] agents."[71]

Human Capital

While the JLET serves as the cornerstone of these changes, human capital improvements serve as the key transforming the culture of the agencies into more effective collaborative entities by instituting joint duty assignments and professional education reforms. These changes target key deficiencies that have created ambiguities associated with the roles and responsibilities within the interagency working environment of the DOJ and DHS agencies. Similar ambiguities existed within the DOD inter service community prior to GNA reforms in 1986, and those changes helped transform weaknesses into strengths for the military. The first reform will require a joint duty assignment for all personnel who reach the mid-management level (GS-15), and will be a condition for advancing to the Senior Executive Service (SES) level. Joint duty requirements will entail a six-month period of assignment at one of the agencies (ATF, DEA, FBI, or DHS) and provide for an educational experience outside the employee's home agency.

The second human capital reform entails new education requirements. Relevant to past lessons, initial changes resulting from the GNA were important but did not fully realize more effective educational reforms until a special board, the Skelton Panel, did so in 1989. The Skelton Panel called for a system that raised standards in order to promote "premiere [U.S.] armed forces," and promote "more emphasis on jointness…not by the four services doing their own thing."[72] In this same spirit, reforms for the DOJ and DHS agencies will incorporate educational requirements that span from the entry level to the senior executive ranks in three areas. The first area consists of a training requirement for all entry-level personnel that will provide education on the roles and responsibilities of the joint agencies and be provided internally by the respective participants' home agency.

The next area will require all persons entering a supervisory position to receive advanced training in joint operations and investigations during a one-week interagency course. This course must also include "hands-on exercises," similar to those instituted by DOD, that will prepare the supervisor to operate in a joint DOJ-DHS environment.[73] The third area will require all SES-level personnel to participate in a one-week course delivered in an interagency setting, relating to strategic-level topics associated with joint agency operations and investigations. As a final note, the JLET must be incorporated in the development and approval of joint training curricula and exercises.

Resource Capital

The final set of reforms will require changes of resource capital components within the joint agencies in order to promote more effective and cost efficient solutions in two areas:

training academy resources and the acquisitions processes. In both areas, a special inter-departmental (DOJ-DHS) committee must be assembled in order to perform a study and recommend practical reforms. Additionally, the committee must answer to the JLET who will be answerable to the department heads and ultimately to Congress. Each of the four agencies operates its own academy, therefore the committee in its review of this area, will make recommendations to consolidate training academies to one location, where they will be able to share space and rotate instructors.

Finally, the special committee's study will focus on current acquisition processes employed by each of the agencies and recommend broad-level joint acquisitions solutions. This portion of the study will focus on all major acquisitions including but not limited to information technology resources such as information-sharing systems and associated maintenance and development costs; educational supplies and materials needed at the academies; all office supplies (computer printer ink cartridges, paper, pens, etcetera); and other acquisition needs.

Conclusion

The HSA in 2002 merged 22 separate agencies into the DHS and was caused to harmonize the functions of key aspects of the nation's protection. More than 10-years after the Homeland Security Act of 2002 authorized the creation of DHS, however the United States of America (U.S.) is faced with evolved threats connected to transnational and domestic crime and terrorism. Constrained government budgets for the long-term and a looming national debt characterize today's economic climate, a factor that will require greater interagency efficiency. U.S. federal law enforcement agencies—including ATF, DEA, FBI, and ICE (HSI)—all complement the national security model. Each of the four agencies confronts common threats—

including those posed by terrorism and significant transnational and domestic criminal organizations—that constitute unique dangers to the U.S. from outside and inside its borders.

To manage successfully twenty-first century challenges the DOJ and DHS Federal law enforcement agencies must undergo legal reforms including, organizational changes and modernize its administration. Decades of Department of Defense reforms provide valuable lessons regarding what has and what has not worked, and suggests a framework to enhance unity of effort between the DOJ and DHS. In order to address organizational deficiencies and modernize its administration, Congressional reforms among the DOJ and DHS agencies must comprise improvements to the following areas: Organizational Capital, Human Capital, and Resource Capital.

Bibliography

Bolton, M. Kent. *U.S. National Security and Foreign Policymaking After 911: Present at the Re-Creation*. Lanham: Rowman & Littlefield Publishers, 2008.

Bush, George W. *Decision Points*. 1st ed. New York: Crown Publishers, 2010.

Cheney, Richard B., Bill Taylor, and CSIS Study Group on Professional Military Education. *Professional Military Education: An Asset for Peace and Progress*. Panel report. Washington, D.C.: The Center for Strategic & International Studies, 1997.

Daly, John Charles, George S. Brown, and American Enterprise Institute for Public Policy Research. *The Role of the Joint Chiefs of Staff in National Policy: A Round Table Held on August 2, 1978, and Sponsored by the American Enterprise Institute for Public Policy Research*. AEI forum 21. Washington, DC: Aei, 1978.

Deflem, Mathieu. *The Policing of Terrorism: Organizational and Global Perspectives*. Criminology and justice studies series. New York: Routledge, 2010.

Dillon, Anthony E. "Administration of U.S. Federal Law Enforcement: Why There is a Need for Federal Law Enforcement Reform Legislation." Master's Thesis, Marine Corps University, 2009.

Franco, Celinda. "The MS-13 and 18th Street Gangs: Emerging Transnational Gang Threats." Congressional Research Service. Washington, DC: 2010.

Freeh, Louis J., and Howard B. Means. *My FBI: Bringing Down the Mafia, Investigating Bill Clinton, and Fighting the War on Terror*. 1 St Martin's Griffin ed. New York: St. Martin's Press, 2005.

Friedman, Thomas L. *The World is Flat: A Brief History of the Twenty-First Century*. Rev pbk ed. New York, NY: Picador, 2007.

Hamilton, Alexander, James Madison, John Jay, Clinton Rossiter, and Charles R. Kesler. *The Federalist Papers*. New York, N.Y.: Mentor, 1999.

Library Of Congress. Federal Research Division. "Organized Crime and Terrorist Activity in Mexico, 1999-2002." Washington, DC: Library of Congress, 2003. http://www.loc.gov/rr/frd/pdf-files/OrgCrime_Mexico.pdf (accessed on January 17, 2012).

Locher, James R. III. "The Goldwater-Nichols Act 10 Years Later: Taking Stock of Goldwater-Nichols." *Joint Forces Quarterly*, (Autumn 1996): 10-16.

———. "Has it Worked? the Goldwater-Nichols Reorganization Act." *Naval War College Review* 54, no. 4 (Autumn 2001): 95-114.

Markson, Jerry. "FBI, ATF Battle for Control of Cases." *The Washington Post*, May 10, 2008, http://www.washingtonpost.com/wp-dyn/content/article/2008/05/09/AR2008050903096.html?nav=emailpage (accessed on December 15, 2011).

Mayor, Matt, and Scott Erickson. "Changing Today's Law Enforcement Culture to Face 21st. Century Threats." *Backgrounder, the Heritage Foundation*, no. 2566 (July 23, 2011).

Miroff, Nick. "Drug Gangs Influence Feared in Mexican Vote." *Washington Post*, January 16, 2012. A1.

Mueller, Robert, Congressional testimony. U.S. Congress. Senate. Committee on Judiciary. *Sen. Patrick J. Leahy Holds Hearing of FBI Oversight*, December 14, 2011. Transcripts by CQ Transcripts, LLC,1. http://www.lexisnexis.com/en-us/home.page.

National Commission on Terrorist Attacks upon the United States, Thomas H. Kean, and Lee Hamilton. *The 911 Commission Report: Final Report of the National Commission on Terrorist Attacks upon the United States*. Official government ed. Washington, DC: National Commission on Terrorist Attacks upon the United States : For sale by the Supt. of Docs., U.S. G.P.O., 2004.

National Gang Intelligence Center. *2011 National Gang Threat Assessment*. Washington, DC: October 21, 2011: Federal Bureau of Investigation. http://www.fbi.gov/news/pressrel/press-releases/2011-national-gang-threat-assessment-issued (accessed on December 14, 2011).

President. "National Security Strategy, May 2010." (Washington, DC: Whitehouse, May 2010). http://www.whitehouse.gov/sites/default/files/rss_viewer/national_security_strategy.pdf.

Public Law 99-433, *"Goldwater-Nichols Department of Defense Reorganization Act of 1986"*. Vol. 100 STAT. Washington, D.C.

Public Law 107-296, Title XI. Subtitle C. *Safe Explosives Act*.

Reagan, Ronald, and Douglas Brinkley. *The Reagan Diaries*. New York: Harper Collins, 2007.

Rittgers, David. "Abolish the Department of Homeland Security." *Policy Analysis*, no. 683 (Washington, DC: CATO Institute, 2011). http://www.cato.org/pubs/pas/PA683.pdf.

Seeley, Mark T. *"The Goldwater-Nichols Department of Defense Act of 1986: Genesis and Postscript."*. Masters Thesis, Naval Postgraduate School, 1987.

Stevenson, Charles A. "The Story Behind the National Security Act of 1947." *Military Review* 88, no. 3 (Fort Levenworth: May/Jun 2008): 13, http://www.dtic.mil/cgi-bin/GetTRDoc?AD=ADA499930.

Truman, Harry S. *Memoirs by Harry S. Truman, Years of Trial and Hope 1946-1952.* Kansas City ed. vols2. Garden City, N.Y.: Doubleday, 1955; 1956.

U.S. Bureau of Alcohol, Tobacco, Firearms and Explosives. Available from: http://www.atf.gov/ (accessed January 1, 2012).

U.S. Congress. House. Committee on Armed Services. Oversight and Investigations Subcommittee. *Another Crossroads?: Professional Military Education Two Decades After the Goldwater-Nichols Act and the Skelton Panel.* Washington, D.C.: U.S. G.P.O, 2010.

U.S. Customs and Border Protection. Available from: http://www.cbp.gov/ (accessed January 10, 2012).

U.S. Department of Homeland Security. Available from: http://www.dhs.gov/index.shtm.

U.S. Department of Homeland Security, Office of Inspector General, "Coordination Between FBI and ICE on Investigations of Terrorist Financing," Washington, DC: U.S. Department of Homeland Security, Office of Inspector General, July 2007.

U.S. Department of Justice. *Former Leader of Arellano-Felix Organization Pleads Guilty.* Washington DC: Department of Justice, 2012. http://www.justice.gov/usao/cas/press/2012/cas12-0104-BenjaminArellano-Felix.pdf (accessed January 8, 2012).

———. Available from: http://www.justice.gov/.

———. *Crime in the United States, 2009.* Washington, DC: September 2010: Department of Justice, Federal Bureau of Investigation, Criminal Justice Information Services Division, http://www2.fbi.gov/ucr/cius2009/about/crime_summary.html (accessed on January 22, 2012).

U.S. Department of Justice, Office of the Inspector General. *Explosives Investigations Coordination between The Federal Bureau of Investigation and The Bureau of Alcohol, Tobacco, Firearms and Explosives.* Washington, DC: U.S. Department of Justice, Office of the Inspector General, October 2009. http://www.justice.gov/oig/reports/plus/a1001.pdf (accessed on December 14, 2011).

———. *Review of ATF's Project Gunrunner.* Washington, DC: U.S. Department of Justice, Office of the Inspector General, November 2010, http://www.justice.gov/oig/reports/ATF/e1101.pdf (accessed on December 14, 2011).

U.S. Department of State. *The Merida Initiative: Expanding the U.S./Mexico Partnership.* Washington, DC: U.S. Department of State, March 3, 2011. http://www.state.gov/documents/organization/158009.pdf (accessed on December 14, 2011).

U.S. Drug Enforcement Administration, "Drug Enforcement Administration: 1970-1975," http://www.justice.gov/dea/pubs/history/1970-1975.pdf (accessed January 10, 2012).

U.S. Federal Bureau of Investigation, available on: http://www.fbi.gov/.

U.S. Government Accountability Office. *COMBATTING GANGS: Better Coordination and Performance Measurement would Help Clarify Roles of Federal Agencies and Strengthen Assessment of Efforts.* Washington, DC: U.S. Government Accountability Office, July 2009, http://www.gao.gov/assets/300/292967.pdf (accessed on December 14, 2011).

———. Combating Terrorism: Law Enforcement Agencies Lack Directives to Assist Foreign Nations to Identify, Disrupt, and Prosecute Terrorist. Washington, DC: U.S. Government Accountability Office, May 2007, http://www.gao.gov/products/GAO-07-697 (accessed on January 20, 2012.).

———. *DOJ could Improve its Process for Identifying Disagreements among Agents.* Washington, DC: U.S. Government Accountability Office, April 2011, http://www.gao.gov/assets/320/317573.pdf (accessed on December 14, 2011).

———. "Ensuring Effective Law Enforcement Coordination." *Washington DC: Government Accountability Office* (2009-2011), http://www.gao.gov/highrisk/agency/doj/ensuring-law-enforcement-coorination.php (accessed on December 15, 2011).

———. *Federal Agencies have Implemented Central American Gang Strategy but could Strengthen Oversight and Measurement of Efforts.* Washington, DC: April 23, 2010: U.S. Government Accountability Office, http://www.gao.gov/products/GAO-10-395 (December 15, 2011).

———. "Long-Term Budget Outlook: Saving our Future Requires Tough Choices Today." (Washington, DC: Government Accountability Office, 2007). http://www.gao.gov/assets/120/115126.pdf (accessed on December 14, 2011).

———. MÉRIDA INITIATIVE: *The United States has Provided Counternarcotics and Anticrime Support but Needs Better Performance Measures.* Washington, DC: U.S. Government Accountability Office, July 21, 2010, http://www.gao.gov/products/GAO-10-837 (accessed on December 14, 2011).

———. "The Federal Government's Long-Term Fiscal Outlook, Fall 2011 Update." (Washington, DC: Government Accountability Office, 2011). http://www.gao.gov/assets/590/585881.pdf (accessed on December 14, 2011).

———. *U.S. Efforts to Combat Arms Trafficking to Mexico Face Planning and Coordination Challenges.* Washington, DC: U.S. Government Accountability Office, June 2009, http://www.gao.gov/assets/300/291223.pdf (accessed on December 14, 2011).

U.S. Immigrations and Customs Enforcement. Available from, http://www.ice.gov/ (accessed January 10, 2012).

Endnotes

[1] "The Constitution of the United States of America As Agreed Upon by the Convention, September 17, 1787," (Collated with the Federalist Papers), in Hamilton, Alexander, James Madison, and John Jay. *The Federalist Papers*, ed. Clinton Rossiter. (Penguin Group (USA) Inc., 1961), 542.

[2] George W. Bush, *Decision Points* (New York: Crown Publishers, 2010), 156.

[3] U.S. Government Accountability Office, "Ensuring Effective Law Enforcement Coordination, 2009-2011," http://www.gao.gov/highrisk/agency/doj/ensuring-law-enforcement-coorination.php (accessed on December 15, 2011).

[4] John Jay, "Federalist No. 3," in Hamilton, Alexander, James Madison, and John Jay, *The Federalist Papers*, ed. Clinton Rossiter. (Penguin Group (USA) Inc., 1961), 36. Introduction and Notes. Chares R. Kesler. 1999.

[5] President, "National Security Strategy, May 2010." (May 2010), in letter accompanying report, http://www.whitehouse.gov/sites/default/files/rss_viewer/national_security_strategy.pdf (accessed on January 17, 2012).

[6] Ibid.

[7] Library of Congress, "Organized Crime and terrorist Activity in Mexico, 1999-2002" (Washington, DC: Library of Congress, Federal Research Division, 2003), 1-2, http://www.loc.gov/rr/frd/pdf-files/OrgCrime_Mexico.pdf (accessed on January 17, 2012).

[8] U.S. Government Accountability Office, *Long-Term Budget Outlook: Saving Our Future Requires Tough Choices Today* (Washington, DC: Government Accountability Office, 2007), 1, http://www.gao.gov/assets/120/115126.pdf (accessed on December 14, 2011).

[9] U.S. Government Accountability Office, *The Federal Government's Long-Term Fiscal Outlook, Fall 2011 Update* (Washington, DC: Government Accountability Office, 2007), 1, http://www.gao.gov/assets/590/585881.pdf (accessed on December 14, 2011).

[10] The United States Department of Justice. "Overview." http://www.justice.gov/jmd/mps/manual/overview.htm (accessed on January 1, 2012).

[11] The Bureau of Alcohol, Tobacco, Firearms and Explosives, Mission, http://www.atf.gov/about/mission/ (accessed on January 2, 2012).

[12] The Bureau of Alcohol, Tobacco, Firearms and Explosives. "From the Archives – The Badge Tells the Story," http://www.atf.gov/press/releases/2008/12/122908-historical-badges-tell-story.html (accessed on January 1, 2012).

[13] The Bureau of Alcohol, Tobacco, Firearms and Explosives. "History of ATF from Oxford University Press Inc.—from 1789-1998." http://www.atf.gov/about/history/atf-from-1789-1998.html (accessed on January 2, 2012).

[14] Safe Explosives Act, P.L. 107-296, Title XI. Subtitle C.

[15] Department of Justice, *Former Leader of the Arellano-Felix Organization Pleads Guilty*, by Laura Duffy, (Washington, DC: Department of Justice, 2012) http://www.justice.gov/usao/cas/press/2012/cas12-0104-BenjaminArellano-Felix.pdf (accessed January 8, 2012).

[16] U.S. Drug Enforcement Administration, "History," http://www.justice.gov/dea/history.htm (accessed on January 10, 2012).

[17] U.S. Drug Enforcement Administration, "Drug Enforcement Administration 1970-1975," (Arlington, VA: Drug Enforcement Administration), 4,

http://www.justice.gov/dea/pubs/history/1970-1975.pdf

[18] Ibid, 5.

[19] Federal Bureau of Investigation, "Quick Facts," http://www.fbi.gov/about-us/quick-facts (accessed on January 10, 2012).

[20] Ibid.

[21] Ibid.

[22] Federal Bureau of Investigation, "History: A Brief History of the FBI," http://www.fbi.gov/about-us/history/brief/brief-history/brief-history (accessed on January 10, 2012).

[23] Ibid.

[24] Ibid.

[25] Ibid.

[26] Ibid.

[27] Ibid.

[28] Ibid.

[29] Department of Homeland Security, "History," http://www.dhs.gov/xabout/history/ (accessed on January 10, 2012).

[30] George W. Bush, *Decision Points* (New York: Crown Publishers, 2010), 156.

[31] Department of Homeland Security, "Our Mission," http://www.dhs.gov/xabout/our-mission.shtm (accessed on January 10, 2012).

[32] Ibid.

[33] David Rittgers, "Abolish the Department of Homeland Security," *Policy Analysis*, no. 683, (Washington, DC, CATO Institute, 2011), 1-5, http://www.cato.org/pubs/pas/PA683.pdf.

[34] Immigrations and Customs Enforcement, "About Ice," http://www.ice.gov/about/overview/ (accessed on January 10, 2012).

[35] Ibid.

[36] Ibid.

[37] Ibid.

[38] Customs and Border Protection, "History" http://www.cbp.gov/xp/cgov/about/history/ (accessed on January 14, 2012).

[39] Customs and Border Protection, "U.S. Customs TODAY," http://www.cbp.gov/xp/cgov/about/mission/ (accessed on January 14, 2012).

[40] Charles A. Stevenson, "The Story Behind the National Security Act of 1947," *Military Review* 88, no. 3 (May-June 2008): 13, http://usacac.army.mil.

[41] Ibid, 14.

[42] Harry S. Truman, *Memoirs of Harry S. Truman, Years of Trial and Hope 1946-1952*, vol. 2 (Garden City, NY: Doubleday and Company, Inc., 1956), 46.

[43] Ibid, 51 – 53.

[44] John Charles Daly and others, and American Enterprise Institute for Public Policy, *The Role of the Joint Chiefs of Staff in National Policy: A Round Table Held on August 2, 1978*, ed. transcript, AEI forums. (Washington DC: American Enterprise Institute for Public Policy Research, 1978), 2.

[45] Mark T. Seeley, "The Goldwater - Nichols Department of Defense Act of 1986: Genesis and Postscript," (Master's Thesis, Naval Postgraduate School, 1987), 46-64.

[46] James R. Locher III, "Has it Worked? The Goldwater-Nichols Reorganization Act," *Naval War College Review* 54, Iss. 4. (Autumn 2001): 99.

[47] Goldwater - Nichols Department of Defense Reorganization Act of 1986, Public Law 99-433 (100 STAT. 993-994), 99th Congress.

[48] Norman Schwarzkopf, quoted in James R. Locher III, "The Goldwater-Nichols Act Ten Years Later: Taking Stock of Goldwater-Nichols." *Joint Forces Quarterly*. (Autumn 1996): 12.

[49] National Gang Intelligence Center, key findings from: "2011 National Gang Threat Assessment," (Washington, DC: U.S. Federal Bureau of Investigation, October 21, 2011), http://www.fbi.gov/news/pressrel/press-releases/2011-national-gang-threat-assessment-issued (accessed on December 14, 2011).

[50] Ibid.

[51] Government Accountability Office, "COMBATING GANGS: Better Coordination and Performance Measurement Would Help Clarify Roles of Federal Agencies and Strengthen Assessment of Efforts" (Washington, DC: Government Accountability Office), 47-48 http://www.gao.gov/assets/300/292967.pdf (accessed on December 14, 2011).

[52] Ibid.

[53] Government Accountability Office, "DOJ Could Improve its Process for Identifying Disagreements among Agents,'' (Washington, DC: Government Accountability Office), 49 http://www.gao.gov/assets/320/317573.pdf (accessed on December 14, 2011).

[54] Ibid, 28.

[55] Ibid, 3.

[56] Ibid, 9-17.

[57] Ibid, 9.

[58] Celinda Franco, "The MS-13 and 18th Street Gangs: Emerging Transnational Gang Threats," (Washington, DC: Congressional Research Service, January 22, 2010), 15-16.

[59] Nick Miroff, Drug gangs influence on feared in Mexican vote," Washington Post, January 16, 2012, A1-A10.

[60] Government Accountability Office, "U.S. Efforts to Combat Arms Trafficking To Mexico Face Planning and Coordination Challenges," (Washington, DC: Government Accountability Office, June 2009), 9, http://www.gao.gov/assets/300/291223.pdf (accessed on December 14, 2011).

[61] Jerry Markson, "FBI, ATF Battle for Control Of Cases," *The Washington Post*, May 10, 2008, http://www.washingtonpost.com/wp-dyn/content/article/2008/05/09/AR2008050903096.html?nav=emailpage (accessed on December 15, 2011).

[62] Ibid.

[63] U.S. Department of Justice, Office of the Inspector General, "Explosives Investigations Coordination Between the Federal Bureau of Investigation and the Bureau of Alcohol, Tobacco, Firearms and Explosives," ii-99, http://www.justice.gov/oig/reports/plus/a1001.pdf (accessed on December 14, 2011).

[64] Ibid, v.

[65] Markson.

[66] Ibid.

[67] Matt Mayor and Scott Erickson, "Changing Today's Law Enforcement Culture to Face 21st. Century Threats," Backgrounder, no 2566, (The Heritage Foundation: June 23, 2011), 2.

[68] Robert Mueller, Congressional testimony, Senate Committee on Judiciary. *Sen. Patrick J. Leahy Holds Hearing of FBI Oversight*, December 14, 2011, Transcripts by CQ Transcripts, LLC, 16-17, http://www.lexisnexis.com/en-us/home.page.

[69] U.S. Government Accountability Office, "Combating Terrorism: Law Enforcement Agencies Lack Directives to Assist Foreign Nations to Identify, Disrupt, and Prosecute Terrorists," (Washington, DC: May 2007), 12. http://www.gao.gov/products/GAO-07-697 (accessed on January 20, 2012.).

[70] Richard Chaney and Bill Taylor, *Professional Military Education: An Asset for Peace and Progress*, *A Report of the CSIS Study Group on Professional Military Education*, (Washington: DC, The Center for Strategic and International Studies March, 1997), 51.

[71] Government Accountability Office, "DOJ Could Improve its Process for Identifying Disagreements among Agents,'' (Washington, DC: Government Accountability Office), 1. http://www.gao.gov/assets/320/317573.pdf (accessed on December 14, 2011).

[72] Chaney, 51-52.

[73] U.S. Congress. House. Committee on Armed Services. Oversight and Investigations Subcommittee. *Another Crossroads?: Professional Military Education Two Decades After the Goldwater-Nichols Act and the Skelton Panel*. (Washington, D.C.: U.S. G.P.O, 2010), 31.

www.ingramcontent.com/pod-product-compliance
Lightning Source LLC
Chambersburg PA
CBHW081811170526
45167CB00008B/3400